Change Management for Beginners

Understanding change processes and actively shaping them

by Steffen Lobinger

Table of Contents

1. What Is Change Management?

We live in a time in which our working and living environments are changing at a rapid pace. This affects our personal lives when it comes to changing workplaces and locations, but even more so companies and organizations. Their markets, customers and suppliers are constantly changing, and those who are unable to adapt quickly enough can quickly become losers.

In order to adapt, you have to be prepared to change. But that's easier said than done. This is not easy for many employees but also for members of management. This book should help you to prepare and successfully implement changes in a company or organization.

Change management is above all the preparation of change processes. It is important that you know the different forms that can represent a change.

1. Change in size: Your company may have just made a great deal, but as a result you'll either have to produce a lot more or you'll have to increase your size dramatically. This is not only a logistical and financial problem but will also affect the corporate culture.

2. Changes in the personnel structure: It happens again and again that new faces emerge within the management or that department heads become team leaders within the framework of "Flache hierarchy Projektes". Sometimes a new managing director joins the company and brings his own people with him; however, it means change, and a company will have to prepare for it.

3. Technological changes: Every company will have to update its IT infrastructure at some point, which can lead to serious changes (and a lot of resistance). But perhaps new technology will be introduced, for example mobile apps for the field service or RFID chips for the pallets in the warehouse. Here, change man-

agement is primarily about preparing users well and training them accordingly.

4. Changes in processes: Whether through the introduction of new IT or restructuring, companies are experiencing changes again, for example in business processes or services for customers. It must be taken into account that employees may have to be retrained, that customers may have to be involved, and that the business model, for example, also has to be updated.

5. Changes due to new legal regulations: If the legislator decides to issue new provisions that affect a company, you cannot change that. But you can prepare yourself for such cases because they will always exist. Examples include the banning of chlorofluorocarbons from refrigerators and the introduction of the catalyst.

These are just some of the most common reasons why a company changes. What they all have in common is that they need a certain process to control these changes. This is exactly what change management makes possible.

In this book, we will also look at change management within project management, especially the areas where team leaders and stakeholders are challenged. Because even with projects you can face the same problems and challenges as in a normal company. In classic project management, change management is used to make changes to the project itself. This is a special form of change management, which is dealt with again at the end of the book. The boundaries are often blurred because every change process is usually designed as a project, and it is also important in projects that people accept the project at the end.

2. The Challenges

If you want to change something, it's not easy. You will be able to confirm this yourself if you try to change something in your life but simply can't get your act together or you tell yourself the situation as it is now is "okay".

Organizations consist of people and therefore it is not surprising that there are similar reservations and resistances. The big challenge in change management is not the change itself but how it can be implemented. There will be several challenges you will have to face.

Well meant is not always well done

Despite its good intentions, a change can sometimes take the wrong direction. This happened, for example, with the introduction of seat belts and the legal obligation to use them: Because the car became safer as a result, people drove faster and the number of road fatalities increased for a short time because the injuries were more serious due to the higher speed.[1] This

---

[1] Bjierklie, D. (2006): The Hidden Danger of Seat Belts. URL: http://content.time.com/time/nation/article/0,8599,1564465,00.html [Date of Reference: 10-04-2018]

could only be solved with the help of various campaigns and speed controls. By the way, similar things happened with the introduction of the ABS systems. In the beginning, countless cars flew out of the bend because the drivers thought that the system would already do it —but they couldn't imagine that even the best technology could not change the basic rules of physics.

In change management you will have to deal with all departments of a company but also with customers, suppliers and other affected parties who have to be convinced.

2.1 Top Management

Managers and business leaders tend to demand changes from others that they themselves are not willing to make. A good example was the introduction of email, which was initially ignored by many top managers. They insisted that emails be printed so that they could still write their comments on them with a pen. The editor-in-chief of a daily newspaper, for example, refused to write his own emails. In his opinion, he had a secretary for correspondence.

But it could also be that the management doesn't want to deal with change at all. Let's say you're the head of the IT department and would like to equip your salespeople with better software so they can enter updates on the go. This would speed up the process. But it can happen that the management has no knowledge of IT and for fear of making a wrong decision doesn't make one at all. Later in this book you will learn how to deal with such and the following challenges, but at this point they should only be mentioned briefly.

2.2 Staff

The bigger a company the more resistance you can expect when changes occur. Many employees are satisfied with the job they have and, in particular, they don't want any changes coming from outside. Even those who aspire to a career within a company can resist being suddenly assigned to a new team. Even with small-scale changes, there may always be critics who make life difficult for you in change management.

2.3 Divisions

In many companies, the individual department is a kind of small fortress that tries to ward off enemies. Even without change, it can always come to controversies because department heads do not want to share their areas of responsibility or because they are afraid of losing power and influence—and perhaps even part of their salary. This can also lead you to face a closed resistance group when it comes to the sinecures of a department and employees fear that they will lose some of their current status.

2.4 External Conditions

During a change process, external disturbances can occur again and again. An example could be that in an IT project the suppliers suddenly cause problems and the new computers are not delivered. But it can also be the case that a company that actually wants to grow suddenly gets its credit cancelled, which would be necessary for growth. But sometimes it can also be natural disasters, such as the flood of the century or a hurricane, that can paralyze a company for days on end. This may not often be the case, but it can happen and it would be good if you were prepared for it. **An example** is the **American company Squarespace**, which offers hosting and finished packages of websites. When a storm of the century raged through Hurricane Sandy in New York and the power went out, the generator started, but after a few days the lower floors were flooded and the diesel pumps failed. To keep the servers up and running, staff started carrying diesel cans 17 stories up for hours just to make sure there were as few downtimes as possible.

3. The Requirements

In order for it to be possible for you to change something at all, certain prerequisites must be fulfilled. Not every idea can be implemented, not every change really makes sense. Sometimes you will find that you lack the necessary resources, but sometimes you will also find that there is simply no budget for your project.

3.1 Size and Scope

In order for change management to work, the project needs a certain scope. For example, if you only want to rebuild the office kitchen, you don't have to start a change process. On the other hand, the IPO of a company is a change, but this cannot be achieved with change management alone.

There is no fixed figure that shows when a project is suitable for change management, but there are some factors you can consider.

1. The change must affect several employees.

2. The change is sustainable and not temporary.

3. The change goes through several hierarchical levels.

4. The change is material and relevant to the company.

New T-shirts for the employees in the warehouse affect many people but are not essential. The outsourcing of two employees to another project for a period of two weeks is not sustainable. A suitable example, on the other hand, would be if the management decided to close the field offices and relocate the employees to the head office. Many employees are affected, several departments and areas of responsibility are involved, the change will last at least for some time and is essential for the company.

3.2 Resources

Most changes in a company are initiated as a project, and this project is allocated certain resources, such as employees, premises and a fixed budget. However, change management is not a process that runs within a project but parallel to it and therefore requires its own resources. The introduction of a new software will certainly need trainers, but how exactly the training is implemented in practice can be the task of change management and requires the appropriate skills and manpower to deal with it.

In practice, you will experience that change management and project planning are often seen as a unit. This makes sense because there are overlaps. But change management is all about defining the conditions under which the project can be implemented at all. Therefore it is necessary that you also have the necessary resources for this. Usually only a rather small team is needed for the change management process, but the time and space must also be created in order to be able to carry out the work involved.

3.3 Target Definitions

A clear goal is indispensable for the success of a change process. Vague formulations such as "optimizing the warehouse" or "strengthening the stores" will hardly arouse enthusiasm among employees. The clearer and more specific the changes are formulated, the easier it is to develop strategies to implement them. If, for example, you want to sell the company's products via an online shop, then it is important to specify the corresponding expectations. A well-formulated goal could be: "With our new online shop, we want to increase sales by 10 percent and win 100 new customers per month." The more specifically the goals are defined the easier it is for everyone involved to understand and communicate them.

It becomes more difficult to steer the corporate culture in a new direction. The softer the changes are the more concrete the expected results must be visualized. If, for example, you want to make employees more project-oriented, then it must be clearly stated what you expect from them and how the company, but also the employees themselves, can profit from it. The following definition would be conceivable: "With project

orientation we can serve our customers more effi-
ciently and more personally and the employees benefit
from more freedom and variety. We also expect that
we will be about 25 percent more effective in handling
projects."

4. The Models

The term change management first appeared in the 1960s and was developed from various management theories but also from psychology. Several essential models have emerged that try to describe the topic with different approaches.

4.1 Kotter's 8-Phase Model

One of the best-known models for change management comes from the American professor John Kotter. He teaches at Harvard Business School and runs his own consulting firm based in Boston and Seattle. In 1996, he launched his book, *Leading Change*, which made it into bestseller lists in many countries and made him a kind of guru in change management. In his book he formulated eight phases that need to be considered in a change process:

1. Establish a Sense of Urgency

2. Create the Guiding Coalition

3. Develop a Vision and Strategy

4. Communicate the Change Vision

5. Empower Employees for Broad-Based Action

6. Generate Short-Term Wins

7. Consolidate Gains and Produce More Change

8. Anchor New Approaches in the Culture

According to Kotter, the first step of "demonstrating urgency" is very decisive: Only if the employees concerned understand that a change must take place as quickly as possible will they recognize that there is a necessity. It thus builds up pressure over time, which usually leads to a stronger cooperation.

In addition, a management team must be set up that is prepared to break out of established structures. At this point, you will need to bring together all those who are most likely to make changes and communicate.

Only when the right people are on board can you formulate what you actually want to change in a vision and strategy. The vision must be precise and clear, and the strategy must be adapted to the conditions of your company.

Communicating the change processes in an understandable way sounds easier than it is because on the one hand there will be a lot of resistance and on the other hand the same language is not spoken everywhere. It is therefore all the more important that you formulate the vision in such a way that it can be understood by all participants.

Employees must also be equipped with everything they need for the change process. This usually includes various training courses but sometimes also new offices and computers, in industry possibly also new production facilities and workplaces. In addition, feedback loops are needed to enable employees to communicate with the management team.

In order to maintain morale, some of the goals should be formulated in such a way that they can be achieved quite quickly. These short-term milestones give employees a sense of achievement and at the same time show that they are on the right track. This often allows even doubters to change their minds.

If initial successes are recorded, then these should also be confirmed. If, for example, sales representatives use the new software, they should train their colleagues in it next—so that they can completely switch off the old software.

After all, it's not just a question of achieving the actual goal but also of anchoring the way in which the changes have been managed in the corporate culture. This will be particularly helpful if another change management project is planned in the future.

Kotter's model is considered one of the most widely used. Like every model, however, it also has weak points, one of which is that it always points in only one direction and therefore does not allow any regressions or feedback loops. This model also communicates from top to bottom and initiatives in the opposite direction are not planned.

Kotter developed his model on the basis of Kurt Lewin's ideas.

4.2 Kurt Lewin's 3-Phase Model

Kurt Lewin was a social scientist who is considered the green one of social psychology. He was one of the first to deal with group dynamics and organizational psychology. In 1947, he first described the three phases of change processes in an article. These phases also formed the basis for Kotter's eight-phase model.

These three phases are:

Unfreeze – Change – Defreeze

Since it is not a question of you dealing here with frozen food, here are a few further explanations of the individual phases.

Loosen up

The first phase is about your company and its employees understanding that change is needed. However, you will also have to break down the current status and analyze exactly in which areas the changes are actually appropriate. This serves as the preparation for the actual change phase, the employees have to be questioned and a strategy has to be formulated and communicated.

Change

When all preparations have been completed, all those involved know what to expect and their support is assured, the actual change phase begins. Here it is important that the transition processes are closely monitored and accompanied by those responsible.

Consolidation

In the third phase, the changes achieved must be secured. In this phase it is all about innovations becoming part of everyday life, about the new becoming normal. This process can sometimes take longer than planned.

4.3 McKinsey's 7-S model

When the two consultants Tom Peters and Robert Waterman worked at McKinsey in the eighties, they discovered that there are always similar processes in organizations that run there to generate success. They developed the 7-S model, which is also used for change management.

A distinction is made between soft and hard factors.

The **hard factors** are:

- Strategies
- Structures
- Systems

The **soft factors** are:

- Shared views (Shared Values)
- Abilities (Skills)
- Style
- Employees (Staff)

As a rule, the hard factors are easier to represent, for example as written strategy or as process charts and diagrams, while the soft factors are more difficult to grasp. The consultants were primarily concerned with communicating that all seven factors are interdependent and intertwined.

A new website of a company can serve as an example: It is quite easy to define the target direction, which and how many pages one needs and which IT requirements are necessary for it according to the enterprise strategy. However, the site will hardly be filled with content by the employees if they do not understand to what extent they themselves are affected or if they do not even know how to log in. If instructions are given only as commands from above, this will also be an obstacle. And, finally, you need employees who can work on the project.

This may sound logical at first glance, but these soft factors are often forgotten or underestimated in their importance.

None of these models represent instructions for action but are intended to illustrate the framework in which changes take place. They also do not compete with each other but simply show different approaches and perspectives in order to convey the same.

4.4 Dunphy and Stace's Typology of Change

The two scientists Dexter C. Dunphy and Douglas A. Stace tried a more far-reaching approach: They assumed that no organization is like any other and that therefore there are different ways to approach and implement a change. They also recommend that companies adapt their change strategies to their respective environmental conditions in order to achieve what they call an "optimum fit".

Collaborative style: Collaborative leadership is about involving as many people as possible, especially when it comes to important decisions, both about the future of the organization and about impending change.

Consultative style: The company leaders consult with their employees but not within the framework of a decision-making process, only as feedback providers. The employees have little influence on the decisions themselves, for example when it comes to specialist knowledge.

Direct style: In these companies, people are "governed" from top to bottom, i.e. employees are told what they have to do and there are hardly any opportunities for them to help shape the future of the company. The authority of management is used to implement decisions.

Pressure and coercive style: While with direct style there is at least theoretically still the possibility of contradiction, with pressure style the employees are forced to implement something without being involved in the respective process. The pressure can come from one's own management or from consultants hired for a project.

Based on these different styles, the two researchers formulated appropriate ways to implement change.

Step-by-step changes are most suitable when an organization is already largely modernized, is in the "optimum fit" range and only minor changes are necessary. This is not about quick and comprehensive steps.

Transformation changes can be necessary if a company is outside its "optimum fit" area. In this case it is possible that not only a few small measures but also far-reaching changes are required.

Collaborative change is appropriate when employees and fewer processes are involved. These should be included as early as possible. The same applies if there are many different stakeholders.

The **direct style** is always recommended when great resistance is to be expected yet the changes are urgently necessary. However, it is not suitable for large projects and far-reaching changes because in this case the morale of the employees could suffer greatly.

They derived **five different types of change** from it:

> **Taylorism** - when changes are small but need to be enforced unconditionally.

> **Gradual transition:** When it affects employees and can therefore only take place slowly.

> **Task-oriented transition:** When it comes to new products and new processes.

> **Charismatic transition:** When a change has to be driven primarily by enthusiasm.

> **U-turn:** When a change can only be implemented through the authority of the management, especially in strategic decisions that affect the future of the company.

The models all have their advantages and disadvantages, and each model has also provoked critics. Although they describe methods, they cannot be empirically proven. Nevertheless, they are necessary for you to understand the mechanisms behind a change process.

Let's say your company has to move because the lease was cancelled. A new office is needed, and this will probably cost a little more. How would the models describe such a change?

If you follow the **Kotter model,** then you must first establish urgency (Phase 1), which is rather simple in view of the terminated lease. Next, you need a team planning the move and looking for a new office (Phase 2). It doesn't require a big strategy and vision (Phase 3) but at least an idea of what the new office should offer (for example, better access to the transport network, more daylight, more space, more restaurants in the area, underground parking, etc.).

This must now be communicated and the employees can contribute their ideas (Phase 4). Obstacles may arise (Phase 5), for example employees who will have a disadvantage in the future because they live quite close to the office and this will change or because they will no longer have their own office in the new premises—you will have to overcome these obstacles with long conversations.

In this case, a short-term win (Phase 6) could be to compile a list of the three best properties together or to draw up a list of requirements together. Finally, the new office has to be planned (Phase 7), and after moving in it is important to settle in comfortably (Phase 8).

If, on the other hand, you follow the Dunphy and Stace model, you should first check your leadership style. If decisions are often discussed together with the staff anyway, then you will use a more collaborative style. If time is of the essence and you have already found an office that is as close as possible to your own, then direct style can also speed up the process. However, this procedure can naturally cause more displeasure than if the employees are involved and questioned beforehand.

Of course, you are free to decide if and which model you follow. In practice, you will find that none of the models fits 100% into your change process. Therefore, you will probably use a mixture of all the methods presented.

In most cases, change is not possible without the insight that habits need to be changed. But if you don't want to change yourself and your work, it will be difficult to convince. This is precisely the main task of change management—to motivate employees and take them on a journey.

An **example from Vietnam** shows that **sometimes** it is only possible **with pressure**: In 2008, helmets were introduced there. Although these had actually been in place before, hardly anybody had used them. Now it was announced that from 1 November the helmet obligation would be checked by the police. On 30 October you could still see millions of motorcyclists without helmets in Hanoi and Saigon—one day later, almost everyone had a helmet on. Helpful was the fact that at each crossing resourceful dealers sold helmets. The fear of being stopped by the police and possibly losing their motorcycle through confiscation was so great that it was sufficient to change this behavior. A similar example was the introduction of catalysts for cars and refrigerators without fluorochlorohydrocarbons: Only laws helped to change buying habits sustainably.

5. The Process

The actual change management work takes place before the changes. It is much easier to change something if the necessary preparatory work has been done. This requires a certain process that—similar to project management—describes the path you should take in order to really implement changes. Which of the above mentioned models you use, or even if you use none at all, is not decisive because the process is similar in all cases.

The process describes how changes are planned and implemented but not necessarily when. Usually this is done in a separate project management. The tasks of the change process are to create the conditions for the changes so that they can be implemented as quickly and, above all, as well as possible.
Good change management should be prepared as quickly as possible in its implementation phase.

You will see that it makes little sense to postpone necessary changes, such as switching production to environmentally friendly means, for too long because even during the planning phase the conditions can change if, for example, new technology is introduced.

How long change management takes for a project depends on the project itself. It is usually anchored in the planning phase of the project and then runs as a kind of monitoring process alongside the project work itself or the change measures.

5.1 Problem Definition

Before you even start with change management, you should think about the problem. Is it important and big enough to start a change process? Is it a crucial problem at all and is there a chance to tackle it?

You should analyze and assess the problem very carefully. A change process that is supposed to solve a problem that is too small or too big can have negative effects. If it is too small, the team members will ask themselves why they are wasting their time on it. If it is too big, they will collapse under the burden of responsibility. Very large changes are therefore better divided into smaller projects to ease the pressure.

Here are **some examples of problems in companies** that need change management:

IT problems

Whether it's new software or new hardware, such as RFID readers in the warehouse, companies will always face big challenges when they make changes in IT—just because there is a kind of natural aversion of employees to IT in general. When it comes to IT problems, you should therefore pay special attention to whether—which is usually the case—and to what extent other employees are affected. The installation of an update does not require any change management but the switch to Google Suites does.

Production problems

It will happen again and again that production facilities have to be renewed or even replaced. Even if the emotional resistance is usually lower here, employees must be well trained accordingly. You will have to check very carefully how far the new systems change existing processes. Sometimes, however, it is already enough to want to optimize existing production processes in order to consider change management. In any case, several employees should be affected by the necessity.

Sales problems

Some change management experts say that change is most difficult in sales because the resistance is greatest here. Salespeople usually work very independently and are convinced of their abilities. Changes should therefore be important enough to be able to accept conflicts. This can be new software they have to use or completely new sales techniques and strategies.

An example:

A bank decided to become more customer-friendly. For its branches, this meant no more fixed desks and tasks. Every employee should be able to greet and help a customer coming in—even if only to refer him to an expert. You can certainly imagine the criticism that arose at the beginning.

Organizational problems

When it comes to breaking up existing structures within a company, resistance is almost guaranteed. No one wants to voluntarily leave the little world he or she has built up over the years. The more serious the changes are the more likely it is that change management will be needed.

The following situation can serve as **an example**: The marketing and product development departments are to be merged to improve internal communication. This can mean spatial changes but under certain circumstances also personnel changes. You should be able to explain good reasons for merging these two departments. These can be data or simply convincing findings from daily work.

Problems that come from outside

Very often, problems are not homemade but come unforeseeably from outside. This could be, for example, your main supplier who suddenly goes bankrupt and leaves you without resources or a start-up that tries to conquer your market. Globalization and digital transformation are the biggest challenges facing businesses today. Added to this is instability. But legal or regulatory aspects can also play a major role. If, for example, you want to achieve ISO certification, this will bring snow-covering changes. The obligation in Germany to refer to cookies within websites and the requirement to obtain the consent of visitors was a measure that caused enormous stress, at least for website developers, for a short time—almost all websites in Germany had to be changed.

You can best assess the scope and extent of problems by answering the following questions:

- What do you see as the main problem?

- How did you become aware of the problem?

- Can the problem only be solved through change?

- What is the cause of the problem?

- How many employees do you think are affected by the problem?

- How important is it on a scale from 1 (unimportant) to 5 (very important)?

- How quickly do you think the problem can be solved (days, weeks, months)?

When we talk about problems in change management, we always mean the change process not the project itself.

5.2 Assessment of the Actual Situation

If you think that the problem is big enough or important enough and that change management is needed, then it will be a matter of understanding the actual situation and the extent of the problem. This is an incredibly important step but it is often taken lightly, which can ultimately lead to serious problems.

The transport company Uber had transferred its Southeast Asia business to its competitor Grab (and also secured shares in the company). The basic idea was to have all drivers switch to Grab and also offer their own employees the opportunity to continue working at Grab. It was thought that the offer was so good that no sophisticated change management was necessary. But it didn't work out as expected: some accepted the offer, but others went to a third provider named Go-Jek, who took advantage of the hour and enticed the employees away.

Uber hadn't thought about the needs and wishes of the employees but simply assumed that they would get the same job, only under a new name. But the change the employees saw was that they had to embark on a new corporate culture. For a long time Grab was portrayed as a competitor in a bad light. Go-Jek, on the other hand, was a start-up, too small to be perceived by Uber as important at all. But many drivers saw it differently: they were always told in the past that Grab was bad and they should never work there, so the new start-up was a better option for them.

Even if you think that there are a lot of good arguments for change and they are obvious, it doesn't mean that your employees see it the same way. Besides, even if you believe it, you probably don't know everything that's actually going on in your company. The higher your position, the more likely it is that you will only hear what you want or should hear from your employees.

However, there are several ways to find out what your employees actually want without you having to frighten them. It is advisable to assign someone who is closer to the affected employees than you are.

5.2.1 Polls

The easiest way to obtain a mood picture is to use surveys. You can create a normal survey and send it by email. This has the advantage that you can reach all employees and even oblige them to take part in the survey. The disadvantage is that there are only answers to the questions that have been asked and hardly any comments of your own. There is also the danger that the answers will be overquantified because you are unconsciously looking for majorities instead of analyzing the background of the answers.

If you are conducting surveys, the questions should be well considered. They must not contain any preference. The goal is not to ask what employees think of your idea of change. The goal is to understand whether they see the current situation the same way you do.

A daily newspaper wanted to become more modern and involve the editors more in the online area. "Online-First" was the new strategy. The editors, on the other hand, were used to working towards an editorial deadline in the evening and spending the day researching and editing articles until everything was perfect. That's how they had worked for decades. Now the idea came up to put articles online in the morning. A survey should help to check whether the necessary resources were available. Some questions from the survey:

"Where do you get your information for articles from?"

"When do you get your information?"

"Is all information exclusive?"

"How long does it take to write a 300-word article?"

"What's the first thing you do when you come to the office?"

"How specific is your department?"

From the answers it became clear that some information the news agencies derived was already available in the morning and was also non-exclusive. So it would be easy to put it online right away. Other information, however, especially for exclusive stories, took almost the entire day to be collected. This was why it could not be put online immediately. It also turned out that by closing the editorial office in the evening, the editors usually let the day go slowly at first because they knew that in the end it would be stressful anyway. And almost everyone pointed out that a lot of specialist knowledge was needed in their department.

The newspaper decided—after further surveys and interviews—that the editors should put as much as possible, but according to their own assessment, online, especially non-exclusive material. They organized themselves in such a way that some of them already written articles in the morning and thus had less work to do in the evening. It also became obvious that the references to the necessary specialist knowledge were rather to be attributed to departmental thinking—one did not want to be talked into one's own work by others. As a consequence, editors from all departments were put together in a newsroom so that they could also, but not exclusively, work across departments. However, there were still the "old" desks one could withdraw to when one needed peace and quiet to research and write a comprehensive story.

What you can learn from this is that the questions must be formulated very precisely and you must also be able to interpret the answers correctly.

5.2.2 Interviews

Interviews are a more promising method, especially for small and medium-sized companies. They differ from surveys in that there are fewer participants, but the answers are more detailed and usually of higher quality. If you want to restructure a department with 10 employees, you can talk to all employees.

Interviews should be individual. You can write down questions in advance, but listening is more important. In this phase it is not about hearing the opinion about a planned change but about what your employees think about the current situation. The interviews should therefore be seen more as conversations.

An IT company had the problem that it could not process orders quickly enough and customers were therefore dissatisfied. The company installed Wi-Fi solutions in hotels—the market was big, so was the demand. The CEO called a meeting with all department heads and asked what the problem was. No one could give him an answer. He suggested introducing project management, which he had already bought. After two weeks it turned out that nobody used it and the problems remained the same.

A change management consultant then sat down with the department heads without the CEO but in one-on-one meetings. The question was how the processes were currently. It quickly turned out that the sales staff did not communicate their deals quickly enough to the technicians and the warehouse. That's why there were no routers in stock and the technicians were told the day before that they had to install Wi-Fi in a hotel—which was impossible.

The solution was simple: teams were created from one department each, responsible for several customers. If the salespeople came with a new deal, they immediately reported it to their team, which in turn was able to create the resources for implementation. The survey also revealed that the CEO had too much control in his hands. The warehouse was not allowed to place independent orders but needed the signature of the CEO every time. This in turn turned into a bottleneck, as the CEO was not always in the office. He realized that he had to give his employees more freedom and responsibility.

Patience is required for interviews. Employees often don't have the courage to present the situation to the boss as they feel it. It is therefore highly recommended that these be carried out by external staff. In any case, you should make it clear that it is not a matter of assigning blame but that you have an honest interest in understanding the situation without the honesty of the employees resulting in disadvantages for them. It is up to you whether the interviews will be made anonymous—in a small company the context of the answers will probably make it clear who gave them anyway.

From the above example you can see that it was already sufficient to analyze the actual situation. Try to be as neutral as possible in the conversations. Your goal is not to confirm your views but to get as much information (and other views) as possible.

5.2.3 Focus Groups

The focus group is a kind of group discussion. It is important how the participants are selected for individual groups. In market research, open questions are usually used, but these are presented to several groups in order to ensure partial standardization. In the context of change management, you can use the focus group both internally and externally to analyze the current situation.

For internal changes you should form as diverse a focus group as possible. Try to invite relevant members who can give you the most relevant information. However, a department head meeting is not a focus group. Focus groups are well suited for up to 300 employees. But even with 50 employees, a focus group is still helpful.

Normally, if a change is imminent, you would invite all those who are experts in the field and who deal with the problem on a daily basis. However, the difficulty is that this can quickly degenerate into specialist discussions. It is therefore better to put together a somewhat broader focus group. Take as an example a company that operates several car washes. There is the idea of changing the detergent to a more environmentally friendly one. This would be slightly more expensive but would otherwise have the same properties. Who should be involved in a focus group in this case?

This affects the operators of the plants on-site and the accounting, marketing and sales departments. You should involve an employee from each area but not necessarily the department manager. In addition, it is advisable to select those employees who always have their ear to the ground with the staff. Often these are those who work at the reception, but it can also be the cleaning helper or someone from the accounting department who is simply good with people. In every company there is someone to whom everyone tells everything and someone who tells everyone everything. You search specifically for the first named person and try to avoid having the latter in the focus groups. In this case, by the way, it would also be good to have one or two customers because they can tell you best how the situation is to be evaluated up to date.

Basically, you should always ask your customers how satisfied they are with the current situation when you make any changes that affect them, the service or the product. Focus groups are ideal for this, even if they may not always be representative. One example that shows that customer wishes do not always serve business success is the new coffee shops. Many customers want them to be quiet and comfortable and there should be comfortable seating. The only problem is that these customers sit too long and consume too little. But just knowing the customers' wish was enough to make many cafés today intentionally very noisy—simply to make it unattractive for those who work four hours on their laptops and just order a cup of coffee. Another option, by the way, would be to assign a new Wi-Fi password every hour.

You should now have a good overview of the current situation after the surveys or interviews. Now try again to evaluate your problem: Is it really a problem that concerns your organization, that is important and that needs to be changed or solved? If you answer yes, you can start working on change management.

6. Planning

The analysis of the current situation may have already given you some good ideas about the challenges you will face if you want to push through changes. In an article Ian Gotts, who deals with Sales Force—a customer relationship management company—describes how top executives see change management in their companies in different industries.[2]

64% of respondents did not believe that a change was necessary.

44% had no experience with change management.

44% said that there was no one in management who was involved in the project.

44% said that there were minor wars between the departments.

---

[2] Gotts, I. (2017): The Top 6 Reasons Why Change Fails. URL: https://medium.com/inside-the-salesforce-ecosystem/the-top-6-reasons-why-change-fails-6a105603eeda [Date of Reference: 13-3-2018]

36% said that there was no single reward system for those who implemented and accepted the changes.

31% resisted the threat of downsizing.

And these are, mind you, only those who have admitted these weaknesses. Resistance will come from all areas, from the management and from the different departments, from suppliers, from customers and sometimes also from people who have nothing at all to do with your enterprise.

So the first thing you should do is find out who is affected and who has what reservations about a change. It's about identifying the stakeholders.

6.1 Stakeholder Analysis

Stakeholders are all those who are affected by the change. In a first step, you have to group all of them together:

1. employees who are directly affected

2. head of department

3. external consultants

4. customers

5. authorities

6. interested parties in social media

7. board of directors

8. shareholders

9. journalists

10. competitor

11. family members

12. employees indirectly affected

In the next step, you need to consider what interest these groups have in the change. The best way to do this is to create a table that could look like this—using the example of a new time recording system that is to be installed in a company.

	How/why affected	Which resistances	Which benefits
employees who are directly affected	Everyone has to record time	Nobody wants to say how long he works	Fairer pay-ment when time permits
department manager	Must make evaluations	Even more administrative work	Work per-formance overview
clients	Indirect, when time is measured for customer conversations	Could be given less time to talk to customers	None

You are welcome to continue this table yourself and consider the advantages and disadvantages for the individual groups. First try to fill in these fields your-self. It is also possible to make several entries per field. With the table you get a quite good overview, which you will need for the next step.

The point now is to determine the importance of the various stakeholders. Management may always be important but in some change processes it plays only a minor role and therefore has no great interest in the process. The parking attendant, for example, is often overlooked but can be of great importance when it comes to allocating new parking spaces.

You can build yourself a matrix, as shown in the table below. It consists of the values "Great influence, mediocre influence, little or no influence and unknown" and the significance of the stakeholder "Great importance, mediocre importance, little or no importance and unknown".

It shows that the stakeholders whose influence and importance are highest need the greatest attention. Those with no significance and little influence, on the other hand, can initially be neglected.

A common problem is to define influence and meaning. The implementation of the change is always in the foreground. If many employees are affected, the management of the personnel department is not as important as those persons who are opinion leaders in your company—and that can also be the person at the reception.

You can also add the columns "Meaning" and "Influence" to the table above and then use them accordingly in the table below. If you love numbers, you can also evaluate the two parameters: Meaning is divided into 0-3, 4-7, 8-10 and also the influence. X stands for Uncertain.

	Significance of the Stakeholder			
	Unknown	Little or no Significance	Some Significance	Big Significance
Big Influence	C		A	
Some Influence	C		A	
Little or no Influence	D		B	
Unknown	D		B	

Influence of the Stakeholder (row axis label)

The matrix shows four areas. In field A are all those who have a high influence and are significant for the project. You have to win them over to make the project a success. There are important people in field B, but they have little influence. Above all, they need to be emotionally convinced because they are often the biggest critics. Those who have high influence but no meaning can disturb a project, sometimes they come from outside and just want to express their opinion. You should try to involve them, even if they have no concrete task. Those who have no meaning or influence should not cause you any headaches.

You can also create similar tables by, for example, comparing the stakeholders' interest in the project with the expected resistance or the influence the change will have compared to the resistance against it.

The tables should help you to understand which groups in your organization have which interests and to develop a strategy to address them.

An **example** of an **investment company** should make this happen: The company was a classic investment company but also carried out some investment projects itself, especially construction projects. Previously, the company used email, Excel, Word and a central server to store documents. The security situation was poor, as almost all data could be copied and transferred to a USB stick, for example. In addition, some department heads hardly used any emails or partly dictated them.

The management wanted to modernize the company, not least because it had to be adapted to international standards in order to reach foreign investors. An internal project management system and intranet were planned, all data was to be stored in a central database, and everyone would have certain access rights.

So who had what interests?

The management felt pressure from both inside and outside and wanted to implement the change as quickly as possible.

The investment bankers were concerned about their independence and were afraid of the transparency that a database would bring.

The IT department was enthusiastic but doubted that the staff was sufficient.

The secretaries were pleased that they were getting fewer dictations on the one hand but on the other they also wondered whether this made their job superfluous.

The department, which had already carried out its own projects in the past, pointed out that project management systems had already been used for these and did not want to run two systems in parallel.

The accounting department wanted to know whether the new system could be connected to the existing software.

The legal department raised concerns about employee privacy and pointed out that there were certain standards and norms that had to be met.

Some department heads feared that they now had less monitoring and control because they no longer had to approve so much.

Some employees were happy about a fundamental modernization, which would lead to a stronger identification with the company.

Employees in the field offices were afraid that they would not be considered.

The HR department demanded that the system be available in both the local language and English.

Customers noted that there had to be interfaces to their systems and that it had to be ensured that modernization would not be detrimental to them.

Force Field Analysis

Force Field Analysis is all about identifying the driving and hindering factors. It was also first published by Kurt Lewin. Every change will create resistance, that is a kind of law of nature. But you have to know what kind of resistance it is. At the beginning this list will be quite short, but in the course of the planning it will become longer in both columns. Also here it is a matter of showing you and the team which task lies ahead of you. Often arguments or people from the left column (driving forces) can help to convince opponents.

The Force Field Analysis can also be helpful when it comes to convincing stakeholders or simply explaining the situation to them. In the analysis their interests and positions are also presented.

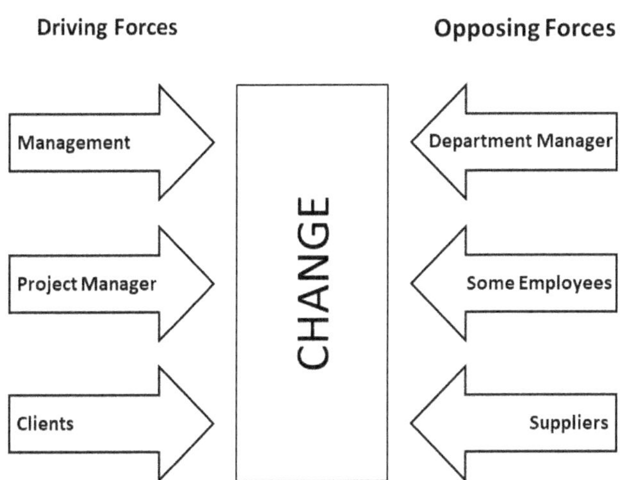

In Force Field Analysis, you list the driving and resisting forces, as in this example.

Example:

The **UN Food and Agriculture Organization (FAO)** introduced such analyses when new reforestation programs were being developed because with such programs there is a danger that the enthusiasm will be great but one forgets what obstacles there may be. Often, economic interests or local political interests are opposed to such programs, but sometimes so are members of the local population and they may even be environmental factors. Many development aid programs fail because the obstructive factors have not been sufficiently taken into account. The FAO went so far as not only to list these resistance factors but also to evaluate them with numerical values.[3] The factors got the parameters "importance" and "strength of resistance". This resulted in a table with the factors at the top that had the highest numerical values. For the FAO, this meant that they had to tackle these problems first.

You won't necessarily have to represent all factors with numbers in your change project but it's good to know that you don't just have to list them; you also have to classify them. The most important and meaningful ones should first come to your attention.

Sometimes the driving factors can also cancel out the resistance factors. For the FAO, one of the driving factors was that fire protection should be improved. This largely eliminated the problems caused by fire damage.

---

[3] ODI (2009): Management Techniques: Force Field Analysis. URL: https://www.odi.org/publications/5218-force-field-analysis-decision-maker [Date of Reference: 15-04-2018]

6.2 Tools in Change Management

As you have already seen, change management works a lot with tables and matrix representations. This is helpful when it comes to basic preparations such as problem solving and stakeholder analysis. But when it comes to the next phase, involving employees in planning, you need some tools that can help.

6.2.1 Mind Maps

Mind maps are best suited, especially if they can be edited by several people. With a mind map, thoughts can be captured first without having to be brought into a structure. This is a great advantage when it comes to capturing stakeholder interests, for example, but also as an accompanying tool in the implementation process. The most popular mind mapping solutions are XMind, which is based on free software, and Mindmeister, which is an online solution.

6.2.2 Flowcharts

The planned changes can be visualized in a flowchart. Often it is a good illustration because it shows the overall picture on the one hand and on the other hand employees can see what effects the changes have on their work and to what extent they are part of the overall project. The problem with flowcharts, however, is that you can quickly get lost in details and the graphic becomes too large and confusing.

But you can also use them to present the current situation and use them as a basis for discussion. A change in customer service can serve as an example here. A company wants to welcome and serve customers who enter a branch differently in the future. In a flowchart you can show very well how a customer is currently received.

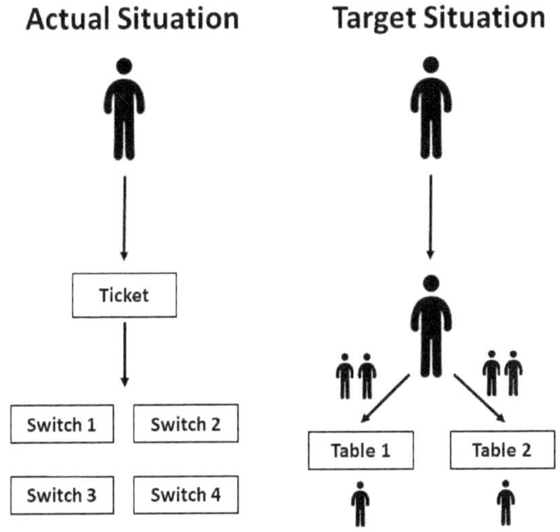

In the actual situation, the customer must draw a ticket and is called to a counter. In the target situation, the customer is greeted by an employee and directed to a table.

Now you can create another chart showing the new process. Thus you have two visually easily understandable representations of an actual and a target state. They are an optimal basis to discuss the planned changes. However, the more complex a change is the less vivid it becomes.

6.2.3 Gantt Charts

Since change management is usually integrated into a project, Gantt charts can also help to get an overview of progress and to check whether important milestones have been reached. However, this requires that you have formulated tasks beforehand. While the project itself is about changing the process, in change management you will rather try to show the changes in the behavior of the employees. It is not so much a question of whether a process has been implemented but whether it is actually being applied. Since these are rather soft factors, it will be more difficult to evaluate them. However, in most cases there is still a key figure, such as the number of employees who are already using the new process.

6.3 Six Thinking Hats

One method to look at a problem from several angles is the Six Thinking Hats method. It was described in 1985 by Edward de Bono in his book of the same name and is still used today in many projects. De Bono assumed that, especially in groups, discussions can lead to misunderstandings because not everyone is on the same wavelength. One example would be that someone has a more emotional argument, while his counterpart looks at things more rationally and analytically. This can lead to ineffective confrontations. In order to create more clarity, de Bono introduced the thinking hats. They have different colors and represent different ways of thinking:

Blue:	Orderly thinking
White:	Analytical thinking
Red:	Emotional thinking
Black:	Critical Thinking
Yellow:	Optimistic thinking
Green:	Creative thinking

Why do you need this for change management? Because it is a good method to solve or uncover problems related to change together. With the Thinking Hats method, the whole group always has the same hat on and only changes the hat color together.

An example:

You work in a garbage truck. The company has big problems with defective trucks and at the same time a high mountain of debts. One of the problems has to be tackled, but should you buy new trucks or pay off the debt first? A group discussion in which all participants wear the same hat can help here. The round with the white hat, for example, talks about what figures and costs are available. The red hat is about disgruntled customers where the garbage is picked up too late. The yellow hat says that new trucks generate quick improvement and more income, and the black hat says that if you buy trucks, the debt level becomes even higher and the company goes bankrupt. The green hat may have the idea of selling a few old trucks, paying off debts with the proceeds and then taking out a loan for new, more effective trucks. The blue hat discusses the overall situation of the company, the market and the competitors.

In most cases, you will call such a round of discussions in the early planning phase of the change process, but it can also be helpful in the ongoing process itself. Even if the changes have been decided upon, the Think Tank Model can serve as a kind of role play. If you play through the change with it, the participants will also be able to understand the changes better. And it can even be that you come to new insights.

6.4 Risk Assessment

There is a certain chance that your plan to change something will fail completely. This can happen during the change process or the whole idea itself may turn out to be a big mistake. This is normal and happens in every company.

For **example**, **Pepsi** thought it was time to redesign the packaging of the popular Tropicana fruit juices. They wanted to become more modern and have a contemporary design. There were a lot of designs, the supposedly best one was selected and production was immediately switched to the new packaging. Customers were first shocked, then angry and finally in turmoil. They wanted their old Tropicana back, and after a month full of bad comments and letters, Pepsi actually rowed back. What they had forgotten was to think about what risk they were taking or, better yet, consider not taking a risk at all.

During the Force Field Analysis you already learned to uncover the forces that work against the changes. In risk assessment, you now try to discover how strong the impact may be if something goes wrong.

The focus is on four questions:

- What is the risk?

- Who is affected by the risk (employees, customers, stakeholders, the public)?

- What happens if the risk event occurs?

- Who is responsible for the risk case?

The latter question is not about the allocation of blame but about the area of responsibility in which the risk falls. Let's assume that your company has to move and someone has decided that you don't need a moving company but the employees can do it themselves. Play this case through: Someone falls down the stairs with a moving box. Who could have prevented that? The person who gave the injured person the box before? The person who made the decision against the removal company? Or the person or body who agreed to the decision to renounce professionals?

For large projects, especially for industrial plants, the risks are of course much greater than for a small change project. Risks are often divided into the following categories:

- Catastrophic

- Very large

- Possible to remedy

- Low

- Negligible

What lies behind this depends on the project in question. In the case of an industrial plant, explosions and heavy falling components are classic catastrophic risks. When programming and implementing new software for customer relationship management, a catastrophic event would be the deletion of all data or a hack that would allow an attacker to access the data.

You should always expect problems to arise and errors to happen. With risk assessment you prepare yourself for the worst-case scenario.

If you have thought about how strong the risks can be, you should consider how big the chance is that they will occur.

There is a likelihood hierarchy from professional risk assessment that can at least serve as a rough guideline:

Rarely - an event arrives only every ten years or less often

Rather rare - an event arrives only every five years

Can happen - an event arrives every two years

Probably - an event arrives every year

Almost certain - an event arrives monthly

As a rule, those events that occur almost monthly are less important than those that occur every five years. Now, you are not going to build a nuclear power plant, so the word risk for your project may be a little exaggerated. But the thought behind it should be clear to you. In particular, software projects can do some damage, especially financial, so they should at least be discussed beforehand.

If your project has big risks, then you should definitely develop mechanisms to detect the risk case as early as possible. A short example shows how a small software and hardware project turned into a huge problem.

A casino had decided to offer its visitors an aquarium where fish and other marine animals swam as an attraction. In order to be state of the art, a thermometer was installed that could transmit the temperature and other water status data to the administration via the Internet at any time. What was not taken into account, however, was that the data was transferred through the same network as all the other data. Hackers exploited the low security levels of the thermometer to gain access to customer data.

Any software project that handles customer data should consider a hacker attack as a possible scenario. How likely this is to happen is a question of judgment. But it is at least a potential scenario. One hotel, for example, considered it a minor threat and therefore invested little in security for a new booking system. It had loopholes, and hackers promptly got access and not only stole data but also deleted it from the server. One sentence you should never say in change management is: "Nobody could count on that," because you can (and should) always count on it.

6.5 What's in It for Me?

This question will be asked by almost every employee who is affected by change. "What's in it for me?" is so important that it has become a framework in its own right and is used under the abbreviation WIFM.

Essentially, this is a further analysis in which the advantages of the changes for all stakeholders are listed. Such a list could look like the following:

Stakeholder	How is he affected?	What advantages does he derive from this?
management	Must release budget	Improves position through cost savings and recognition
department heads	Must make and monitor changes	Change relieves daily work, more time for the essentials

A further column would also be conceivable, which lists what speaks against the change. However, those affected will approach you with these arguments on their own. It is more important that you have arguments that convince them. It depends, of course, always strongly, on which changes are planned. Here are a **few examples of typical changes**:

New accounting software

Pro-arguments for employees: time saving, less complicated, clear overview, less paper.

Teams instead of departments

Pro-arguments: More responsibility, more opportunities to get involved, better communication with other participants, more security by the team, restructuring makes the workplace safer.

Relocation of the company

Pro-arguments: Better working conditions, more parking, public transport connection, coffee machine, shopping facilities, new furniture.

It is indispensable with these arguments that you can put yourself in the position of the respective stakeholder. It is not about selling him facts but about putting yourself in his shoes and thinking about how the changes can help him. Here a renewed look at the

Force Field Analysis is helpful because it gives you good clues as to where the resistance is to be expected.

The ideal situation is reached when all employees see a good reason to support the changes. But this is rarely the case. In a change there will always be stakeholders who have something to lose because their situation, salary or position will deteriorate. For example, the classical doubters, there is no point in "fine speech", you will find it difficult to find something that can change their mind. Ultimately, these are the collateral damages of change that need to be supported. It is at this point that the authority of the management usually comes into play to implement the change. In urgent cases, when an employee is enormously important for the company or a supplier would be difficult to replace, money can help as an argument. However, you should avoid buying the approval and support for a change. It really is the last resort you should use.

7. Execution

You should now have a good plan about what to change and what the goal of change is. You have named the main stakeholders and informed and involved them to the extent that they will support the project as far as possible and that we have minimized the impact as much as possible. Now it's about how you implement all this successfully. Because change management is not only the preparation for a change but also the accompanying of the project and the possible intervention if something goes wrong.

First, you should have a way to measure progress and success. This allows you to check at regular intervals whether the project is progressing as planned or, if not, where the problem might lie. A good tool for this is a simple survey, which you can create using a Google survey document (or any other survey tool). Respondents (preferably all participants) can rate 1 to 10 individual questions/statements. These can be:

- I understand the new model and my role in it.

- I think that the new model will improve our per---formance.

- The management is fully involved when it comes to implementation.

- I know what I have to do to make the new model work successfully.

- I believe that we have the staff and the skills to implement the new model effective-ly/quickly/cost effectively.

- Our colleagues are very committed to implementing the new model.

Of course, these are just a few suggestions that you can or even have to adapt to your respective change project. It is best to use the survey for the first time during the planning phase and then at regular intervals during the implementation phase.

7.1 Plan-Do-Study-Act

You may already be familiar with the "Plan Do Study Act" principle from project management. It is one of the simple models for implementing projects without just stubbornly following a plan. Change management always runs parallel to a project; it is a kind of higher-level monitoring process. The PDSA principle is about you understanding the changes as a kind of circle.

An **example** is a **new maintenance cycle for the trucks of a forwarding company.** It has been shown that more trucks than planned have failed, which has led to discontent among customers but also among employees. The mechanics, on the other hand, fear that they will have more work to do than expected.

Plan

You will first create a new plan, which allows the trucks to come to the workshop once a month for a check (instead of every three months so far).

Do

The first check in the workshop is prepared; there are two trucks a day. At the end, every driver of a truck receives a status report and repair recommendations.

Study

After the first maintenance cycle you should carry out the survey described above and analyze the results. Perhaps it turns out that the mechanics can also check three trucks a day or that you can't check all the trucks in a week.

Act

If the study has shown that changes have to take place, then these have to be worked out and put back into a new plan. The cycle then begins anew.

Of course, the example is greatly simplified. In terms of reactivity, the mechanics will consider in advance exactly how many trucks they can repair. But the point is rather to show that, despite a good plan, new findings and the resulting improvements can always be made. The PDSA method is also excellently suited for small changes that do not require large plans but still have to be carried out properly.

7.2 Test Environments or Entire Organization?

A question that often arises in change management is whether one should first do a test or a test group to confront the change or whether one should apply the change immediately to the entire organization. The answer depends on the one hand on the planned changes and on the other hand on the size of the organization.

You should set up a test environment, for example, if:

- when introducing software, it is necessary to have real users test it in advance in order to see whether the software is suitable for practical use. It would be best to do this during the development phase.

- a fleet of vehicles is to be converted to electric propulsion. Here a test with a few vehicles would provide sufficient data for a complete changeover. But also costs and changes for the running operation have to be considered (e.g. a charging station has to be installed, because of a shorter range there will be disturbances in the operation plan).

- it is project-related work, which should dissolve departments as far as possible. Many companies think that such lean management can increase motivation and save costs. In this case, a test can also help by involving only a few employees from as many departments as possible in a test group.

Examples where a test environment is not required or where there are other reasons for complete implementation:

- An admission ticket for all employees is intended to ensure that only the person who is authorized to do so enters the building. In this case, it is not a problem to change from one day to the next. This applies to most security-relevant changes, especially with regard to building security, but also in industrial production. Legislators also face such challenges: Probably the biggest change project in Germany was the introduction of the euro, which happened virtually overnight. It would have been impossible to introduce only part of the currency.

New rules and processes are also usually introduced as binding for everyone: These can be small things like forms or regulations for expense reports or larger measures like the use of a new logo. Here it is best to avoid using old and new logos at the same time. Especially with name or logo changes, as many media as possible should be served by the change at the same time, even if the stationery has not yet been used up. (With a new logo, change management is primarily about achieving acceptance among employees and explaining why the logo was designed in this way but also discussing, for example, in marketing and IT, which color spaces are used and what the proportions are.)

An **example of a worldwide change** was the so-called **Millennium Bug, or the Y2K problem**. Since until the 1990s many computers only used the last two digits as year numbers, it was feared that once the year 2000 had been reached, computers would interpret the number as 1900. Test environments helped here only within an organization, but nobody knew what further effects there would be. Ultimately, there was no other choice than to switch all computers to the four-digit annual system. It is still not understood, however, whether nothing serious happened on January 1, 2000

or whether the problem was simply not as big as pre-
dicted by many who warned of a disaster.

7.3 Step-By-Step Implementation

Another way to implement change projects is to do it in smaller steps. This is particularly recommended for large, extensive and complex projects. In the software area, you will often see this when it comes to introducing enterprise solutions, for example. These steps can be:

- To introduce only parts of the project

- Integrate only certain user groups

- To be introduced only in phases

The main advantage of step-by-step implementation is that you have much better possibilities to monitor progress and to intervene in time. A hotel consulting firm in Asia wanted to become more professional and, after attending a seminar, the CEO decided to buy and deploy SharePoint, a program that had just come into fashion. His IT staff installed it on all computers and sent each employee their login details by email. It will come as no surprise that nobody used it. But the CEO didn't understand it and sent an angry email afterwards, in which he accused the employees of not wanting to change and of being against modernization. When employees even resigned, he brought consultants on board. They immediately realized that "the earth was already burnt to the ground" and that a company-wide introduction was currently out of the question. They decided to first involve the IT staff, and only with excerpts from the extensive range of programs. When this was successfully implemented, some interested employees in the accounting department had access to selected functions such as the calendar and some folders for documents. Gradually, parts of SharePoint were implemented according to the respective requirements, in each case to the extent that one felt the least possible resistance. And with each new phase, consultants, CEOs and employees learned something new and were able to take it to the next phase.

7.4 The Next 100 Days

As soon as the change process itself is completed, the time of the next 100 days begins. Now we will see whether the changes have really taken hold, whether they are sustainable, and receive the necessary support. It is often said that the first 100 days are decisive. It is a tradition for political leaders to make an initial assessment of how well they are doing in office after 100 days. Some journalists also leave politicians largely alone during this time when it comes to critical questions and issues. In change management it is a rather unwritten (and not really proven) rule that it takes about 100 days to implement a change sustainably without running the risk of regressing again.

Here, too, there is a list of questions that you can use as a tool to monitor this phase:

1. What instruments do you have to check sustainability?

2. Have you set milestones for the first 100 days that document the sustainability of the implementation?

3. Are there feedback loops with the management about the success of the change?

4. Do you regularly create surveys on the implementation of change?

5. Is there a benchmark that determines after 100 days whether the change is sustainable?

6. What plans do you have to be able to intervene with possible problems?

To make monitoring less difficult for you, here are a few tips on which instruments can help you:

You can best determine the sustainability of a change with target/actual analyses. After the introduction, this balance should be balanced, i.e. the target state is at the same time the actual state. It is best to use the list of change goals as a kind of checklist. In the example of the switch to an electric fleet, all cars and trucks should be equipped with an electric drive after 100 days at the latest and sufficient charging stations should be available. Especially with such a change, delays can occur, so that the 100 days are not enough. This also raises the question of whether change management has been completed with the introduction of the first or last vehicles.

7.5 Feedback

The most effective way to determine how the change process is running is through feedback. This can occur in different ways. As already described, you can send a survey to all employees and regularly ask them how the change process is accepted. You can also analyze data, for example whether costs have already been saved, whether more has been produced, or whether a process has become more efficient as a result of the change. But one thing should be clear to you: without feedback there will be no successful change management.

One of your main tasks during the changeover is to motivate employees and stakeholders to give as much feedback as possible. And the feedback should be constructive or at least describe mistakes and problems exactly.

Even with the best preparation, you will not be able to convince all naysayers and they will express criticism again and again during the implementation. That can be exhausting, but on the other hand they sometimes bring in a new view of things.

7.6 The Problem Owner

In the implementation phase, it is important that problems are identified as quickly and early as possible. The best plan does not help if it cannot be implemented at the first obstacle. There are different methods to recognize such warning signals in time. More important, however, is to determine who takes the initiative. In project management, this person is called the problem owner, and this is also a suitable term for change management. The problem owner recognizes the problem, reports it and analyzes it together with the team. Then a solution is worked out and the problem owner monitors that it is successfully implemented.

There is always one employee in a company who has to do everything: The Mr. Someone. When there is a problem, most employees say, "Someone has to solve it." When a manager is faced with a problem, he asks his employees to have someone take care of it. (Mr. Someone has another colleague, Mr. Anyone).

Problems are identified but not solved. It is a question of corporate culture that employees are allowed to take care of a problem. Problem ownership must not end at department doors and titles. Who takes care of a problem must receive the full support of the team, the departments and the management in order to solve it. It is often understood that one is then responsible for the problem. Far from it: one is responsible for the solution but together with others.

How to motivate employees to identify problems and take care of them is a question of corporate culture. Where you punish the bearer of bad news, you will hardly find such a culture. As the leader of a change management project, you should make it clear that uncovering problems is positively encouraged and the problems that are brought to light will be evaluated. Accepting problems should also be career-promoting.

A good problem owner has the following train of thought:

I see a problem, but I don't understand its full extent and I don't know how to solve it, but I am sure that it is important and has to be solved. So I will do everything I can to understand it better and get support and advice to solve it. If I cannot solve it myself, I will take care of it until I have found a more suitable problem owner.

However, you should make sure that there are not always just a few employees who are problem owners and many others who are grateful that they don't have to do the work. Most importantly, employees must understand that even if they can't solve the problem, they won't suffer any disadvantages but will take advantage of it if they identify problems and help find solutions.

Exception-based reporting

There are many different methods to measure progress, and especially in large organizations long reports are written regularly. In these, everything that has happened is documented. Many employees delve into page-long descriptions of their activities. The problem: They want to present themselves well, but it doesn't help the project.

With exception-based reporting, only those things are reported that lie outside a certain standard range. Or to put it another way: The report includes what is not running according to plan. The term is often used in project management but also in retail for loss analysis. In change management, this is a very effective way to identify problems early on and to get a good overview of the progress and problems within a project through the reports.

When planning the project, you should consider which parameters are best suited to describe deviations from the plan. One possible way is to define different categories: Critical, a little critical, very critical (not critical does not appear here because basically only critical problems should be listed).

However, these categories need further definitions, for example whether they are critical for a certain phase, for a certain part of the project, or even for the entire project.

7.7 Performance Ratings

There's an old saying that says, "Only what is measured can be improved." This is not true in all cases; on the contrary, even decisions taken from the gut can be successful, but a good data basis does not hurt. How can you collect this data, and above all derive performance from it? First of all it is about collecting the data.

7.7.1 Data Analysis

In order to see whether changes actually have the effect one wanted to achieve, various data can often help. Especially when it comes to optimizing sales figures, saving costs or gaining market share, you can use the figures to see whether and how the changes will have an effect. However, this means that these figures must also be prepared for this purpose. The pure sales figures do not help you if they are not connected with change management.

An example:

A clothing company decides to switch production from pure cotton to synthetic fibers. This is intended to save costs,but also to take account of the trend towards functional clothing. This conversion requires several change processes: on the one hand the re-equipping of the machines, as well as training of the seamstresses, and on the other hand the marketing. The machines and the employees at the sewing machines will provide data on how high the output is. However, this will probably remain constant because the costs for the material will be saved. Change management must therefore monitor material costs. While these costs change directly, it will probably take some time in marketing and selling the T-shirts for customers to get to know and accept the new product. But seamstresses must also be trained promptly to ensure that they can process the new fabrics properly. It is essential to ask them about this.

So you can see how important it is for change management to request the data that really represent the change.

7.7.2 Progress and Success Control

However, data alone will not help you if it is not put in relation to each other. In order to evaluate change management, the data must be categorized and weighted. The following categories are helpful:

- Sales, unit and production figures

- KPIs

- Audits

The first category has already been mentioned. These numbers are collected anyway, and you can easily incorporate them into your change management performance process. To see if you are successful, you should set benchmarks. It is best to do this in the planning phase by determining how many more products you want to sell or produce. These figures have to be adjusted again and again because you will certainly be a little off at the beginning. The absolute figures are less important than the general trend: Is production going up overall, even if there is a small setback here and there (for example because a problem had to be identified and solved)?

With regard to the KPIs, experts argue about how many such indicators are really needed and whether they actually describe the change. Basically, however, it is a good thing if the success of your change process can also be expressed and measured in figures.

In project management, KPIs are used, among other things, to see how many changes there are and what caused them. In change management you can also apply this. Such KPIs can be:

% of changes implemented

% of employees who underwent a change of direction

Number of workdays/hours per employee used for the change

Number of successfully completed audits

% of satisfied employees (after audit)

% of subsequent changes in the change process

7.7.3 Audits

Even if audits of employees are frowned upon—not without good reason—they can, if used correctly, bring a lot of benefits in change management. When assessing the current situation, you have already learned that surveys can be very helpful in understanding how employees see the situation.

Such surveys are even more important in the change process. Only in this way can you see whether the behavior of the employees has really changed. An audit should be as comprehensive as possible but without consuming too many resources. Therefore you should adapt it exactly to the size of your project. With a small change, it can be enough to create surveys. However, you should not make these surveys mandatory because then you can already see from the number of not submitted surveys how much the change project has already anchored itself in people's minds or whether employees still reject it and therefore do not respond.

Audits should also not take too long, it is more important to gain snapshots. In most cases, you will ask whether the processes that were defined in the implementation plan were carried out in the same way.

7.8 Milestones

Milestones are an almost unavoidable method for measuring the progress and success of a change process. Since change management always consists of projects, it makes sense to use this method from project management. Your challenge will be to define these milestones.

A few examples:
With the introduction of a new accounting software it can be a milestone that the software has been installed on X computers, another milestone that Y em-

ployees have been trained, a third milestone that Z bookings should already be carried out.

A company wants to close its canteen and switch instead to a system where employees can order their lunch online. Here a first milestone is the implementation of the order website and a first survey of a selected test group, another the first menu bar and the feedback of the employees, the next is successful online orders, another milestone the first test orders and the feedback of the users, then the conversion of an entire department to the online orders.

Milestones make the most sense if they are quantifiable, i.e. can be expressed in figures. If software is installed on 20 computers but the milestone included 30 computers, you know you have a problem. Always try to express milestones in numbers. However, there are also projects where this is not always possible, such as the milestone "Website online".

7.9 Rapid Issue Identification

Rapid Issue Identification is a tool that is used primarily in software development but also with machines and in high-risk organizations. This method consists of three steps:

- Discover

- Analyse

- Fix

RII is a process that is permanently running. In software development, for example, a bug is found, then analyzed for its effects, and finally fixed. In a hospital, for example, it can be discovered that ventilation is not sealed in a sterile environment. With the RII it is possible for any employee to uncover the problem and ensure that it is solved. The problem ownership described above can be incorporated, but the problem detector does not always have to lead the solution process. RII is upstream of Problem Ownership and serves as more than an early warning system. Every employee should be able to identify and report problems.

This is particularly important in change management because, despite all planning, it is not always possible to predict all possible effects in advance. So it can happen that you have forgotten (or simply didn't know) that the registration office is currently switching to a new system when switching from diesel to electric cars and that new registrations are therefore delayed by a few days. An employee reads about it in the newspaper, sees that the change process could be affected, and reports the problem immediately. This is the ideal situation. Simply put, the process allows all employees to think along and be vigilant.

7.10 Change Management Checklist

So that you have a little help at the beginning as well as during the running project, now follows a short checklist, which can help you to keep an overview.

- ❏ Is there a definition of the change that is to be made?

- ❏ Is there a clear goal?

- ❏ Is there an analysis of the benefits?

- ❏ Is there a Force Field analysis?

- ❏ Is there a model according to which the change management is to take place?

- ❏ If so, which one?

    - ❏ Kotter

    - ❏ Lewin

    - ❏ McKinsey

    - ❏ Dunphy

    - ❏ Other model

- ❏ Has a team been put together to prepare for the changes?

- ❑ Is the management ready to get involved?

- ❑ Have the possible drivers and preventers been identified?

- ❑ Is there an implementation team?

- ❑ Should the changes be introduced in steps, are these steps sufficiently described?

- ❑ Are benchmarks for the success of the project described?

- ❑ Is there a change monitoring process?

- ❑ Is there an implementation process?

7.11 Personal Checklist

As a change manager you can also ask yourself again and again whether your work is satisfactory so far. This list gives you a few questions that will help you to stay on track.

- ❑ Is my communication understandable and does it reach the people it addresses?

- ❑ Is my team aware of why we're making this change and what the point is?

- ❑ Do I pass on enough information and am I transparent enough?

- ❑ Do my employees have all the necessary information and tools for the change process?

- ❑ Do I intervene fast enough when there's a problem within the team?

- ❑ Do I motivate my team sufficiently?

- ❑ Do I have support in the change process from the management?

- ❑ Am I myself positive about the change?

- ❑ Do I communicate this attitude sufficiently?

- ❑ Am I listening sufficiently to the naysayers and critics?

- ❑ Do I accept amendments positively and do I not reject them directly?

- ❑ Do I radiate competence and am I recognized as competent in the team?

- ❑ Am I setting a good example?

- ❑ Do I support my team in guiding others through the change?

- ❑ Do I make decisions based on facts?

- ❑ Do I continuously check how the change is accepted and implemented?

- ❑ Am I prepared to intervene, even if it prolongs the process?

- ❑ Is the successful implementation important for me or that it happens in the required time?

8. Change Management in Projects

In a project, especially in those that are managed according to the classic waterfall principle, the change management system is a process that describes how changes are made to the project itself. Change management regulates very precisely how a change is applied for, who approves it, how it is verified and implemented, how it is measured, whether it has been successful, and how many changes there are at all.

Even the best planning won't always be able to exist in reality. It is in the nature of projects that they are changed. This is particularly visible in the software industry. Here you can define the framework of a software development and determine which requirements it should solve, but in the course of the project you will see again and again that something has to be changed. Sometimes this may only be small things, like, for example, that certain program parts have to be developed first or fonts have to be adapted, or big problems may arise (e.g. if the requirements for a server were wrongly dimensioned and it has to be upgraded first). While such a problem has a big impact but is rare, your attention should be focused on the small changes because the devil is often in the details: Many small changes can slow down a project considerably or exceed the budget. Think only of a construction project: If a builder gets the idea of having small tiles instead of large ones, this may mean that the existing ones have to be torn out or that the subsequent work cannot be done until the new tiles have arrived. Of course, this also has an influence on the construction costs but also on the mood among the employees.

A small checklist can help to make the extent of a change clear:

- ❑ What exactly is the problem?

- ❑ What influence does it have on the project?

Analysis

- ❑ Is the problem critical, very critical, less critical? Is the change important, very important, less important?

- ❑ Which interfaces and sub-projects are affected?

- ❑ What was the cost of the problem?

- ❏ What is the cost of the problem if it is not fixed immediately?

- ❏ Which employees are affected?

Resolving

- ❏ How should the problem be solved?

- ❏ How long will the process take?

- ❏ What are the effects of the troubleshooting on other processes?

- ❏ What are the costs of the correction?

- ❏ Which employees are affected?

- ❏ Which stakeholders need to be informed?

- ❏ Who is responsible for the repair?

- ❏ What is the timeframe for change?

9. Summary

Change will always meet with resistance, and yet it is often inevitable. A new uniform is quickly designed and purchased, but persuading people to wear it can sometimes take a big effort.

After reading this book, you should better understand how change can be successfully implemented in an organization. Whatever model and method you use, they all have in common that you must first reach the people affected by the change.

Often one is so enthusiastic about an idea that one goes too fast into the implementation without having planned the project properly beforehand. However, good planning helps you to save a lot of time later and also to spare your nerves. The better you identify the stakeholders and their needs the easier it will be for you to win them over to the process.

The "softer" the change is the more important it is. Soft changes are those that affect the culture or certain processes of a company as well as restructurings in management. The more people are affected the more they have to be put at the center of attention.

The tables and graphs mentioned can be a great help and hopefully also the checklists listed at the end of the book. You should now be well equipped to tackle your first change management project. Good luck with it.

Yours,
Steffen Lobinger

Copyright and legal notice

link, no illegal content was identifiable on the pages to be linked. The Author has no influence on the related content. Therefore, the Author hereby explicitly distances himself from the content of all linked pages that have been modified after the link was set. For illegal, incorrect or incomplete content and in particular for damages resulting from the use or non-use of this information, the provider of the page in question, but not the Author of this book, is responsible.

Sources

Bjierklie, D. (2006): The Hidden Danger of Seat Belts. URL: http://content.time.com/time/nation/article/ 0,8599,1564465,00.html [Date of Reference: 10-04-2018]

Gotts, I. (2017): The Top 6 Reasons Why Change Fails. URL: https://medium.com/inside-the-salesforce-ecosystem/the-top-6-reasons-why-change-fails-6a105603eeda [Date of Reference: 13-3-2018]

ODI (2009): Management Techniques: Force Field Analysis. URL: https://www.odi.org/publications/5218-force-field-analysis-decision-maker [Date of Reference: 15-04-2018]